POVERTY ANI

Chris Jones ar

with responses from Mimi A
Dimitra-Dora Teloni and Sanford F. Schram

SERIES EDITORS:
Iain Ferguson and Michael Lavalette

This print edition first published in Great Britain in 2014 by

Policy Press
University of Bristol
6th Floor
Howard House
Queen's Avenue
Bristol BS8 1SD
UK
t: +44 (0)117 331 5020
f: +44 (0)117 331 5367
pp-info@bristol.ac.uk
www.policypress.co.uk

North American office:
Policy Press
c/o The University of Chicago Press
1427 East 60th Street
Chicago, IL 60637, USA
t: +1 773 702 7700
f: +1 773-702-9756
e:sales@press.uchicago.edu
www.press.uchicago.edu

ISBN 978 1 44731 615 2 paperback

British Library Cataloguing in Publication Data
A catalogue record for this book is available from the British Library.

Library of Congress Cataloging-in-Publication Data
A catalog record for this book has been requested.

Cover design Policy Press
Printed in Great Britain by www.4edge.co.uk

OTHER TITLES AVAILABLE IN THIS SERIES

For more information about this series visit: www.policypress.co.uk/crdsw.asp

Policy Press also publishes the journal *Critical and Radical Social Work*; for more information visit: www.policypress.co.uk/journals_crsw.asp

Contents

Notes on contributors

Lead authors

Chris Jones is Adjunct Professor of Social Work at Liverpool Hope University. He has published widely on aspects of social work, social work education and the demonisation of the poor by the state.

Tony Novak was formally a lecturer in social work and social policy at the Universities of Bradford and Liverpool. He has written widely on poverty, inequality and state brutality.

Respondents

Mimi Abramovitz is the Bertha Capen Reynolds Professor of Social Policy at Silberman School of Social Work at Hunter College and The CUNY Graduate Center, US. A scholar and an activist, she writes extensively about women, poverty, the economy and US social welfare policy. She is the author of *Regulating the lives of women: social welfare policy from colonial times to the present*, the award-winning *Under attack, fighting back: women and welfare in the US*, and co-author of *The dynamics of social welfare policy* and *Taxes are a women's issue: reframing the debate.* Dr Abramovitz is currently writing *Gender obligations: the history of low-income women's activism since 1900* and researching the impact of privatisation on the delivery of human services in New York City

Suzanne Dudziak, BA, MSW, PhD, is Associate Professor of Social Work at St Thomas University, New Brunswick, Canada. She writes and publishes on various aspects of social work and social movements internationally.

Dimitra-Dora Teloni teaches social work in the Technological Institution of Patras, Greece. Her research interests cover poverty and social work, community work, anti-racist social work and the link between social work and social movements. She is involved in the local Social Work Action Network in Patras/Greece.

Professor **Sanford F. Schram**, PhD, teaches courses on American politics, political economy, social welfare policy, social theory, and research methodology at Bryn Mawr College, where he has been co-director of the Center on Ethnicities, Communities, and Social Policy. His books include *Words of welfare: the poverty of social science and the social science of poverty* (1995), which won APSA's Michael Harrington Book Award, and three subsequent books on social welfare policy.

Series editors

Iain Ferguson is Professor of Social Work and Social Policy at the University of the West of Scotland and a member of the Steering Committee of the Social Work Action Network.

Michael Lavalette is Professor of Social Work and Social Policy at Liverpool Hope University and National Co-ordinator of the Social Work Action Network.

Series editors' introduction

For much of its history, mainstream social work in Britain has been a fairly conservative profession. It has often reflected the dominant political ideologies of the day, while presenting itself as resolutely 'non-political'. Thus, the first social work organisation, the Charity Organisation Society (COS) (1869), rigorously adhered to the Poor Law notion that the poor could be divided into 'deserving' and 'undeserving', rejected any form of state intervention aimed at improving people's lives (including free school meals and old-age pensions) and saw the practice of individual casework as the best antidote to the spread of socialist ideas.

By contrast, social work in the 1960s reflected a broad social democratic consensus, evident in the recommendations of the Seebohm Report in England and Wales and the Kilbrandon Report in Scotland on the basis of which the new generic social work departments were established. In most respects, the social work of this period reflected a huge advance on the punitive individualism of the COS (and, it should be said, the punitive individualism of our own time). Even then, however, there was still a tendency to pathologise (albeit it was communities rather than individuals that were seen as failing) and to ignore the extent to which statutory social work intervention continued to be experienced by service users as oppressive and paternalistic. Be that as it may, the progressive possibilities of the new departments were soon cut short by the onset of a global economic crisis in 1973 to which the Labour governments of the time could offer no answer, except cuts and belt-tightening.

What is also true, however, as we have argued elsewhere (Lavalette and Ferguson, 2007), is that there has always been another tradition in social work, an activist/radical approach which has sought to present an alternative vision both to individualism and also to paternalist, top-down collectivism. This approach, which flourished in the UK in the 1970s, located the problems experienced by those who sought social work support in the material conditions of their lives and attempted to develop practice responses that challenged these conditions and their effects.

One source of theory underpinning that approach was the excellent series Critical Texts in Social Work and the Welfare State, edited by Peter Leonard and published by Macmillan.

Three decades on, this current series aims to similarly deepen and refresh the critical and radical social work tradition by providing a range of critical perspectives on key issues in contemporary social work. Social work has always been a contested profession but the need for a space for debate and discussion around ways forward for those committed to a social work practice informed by notions of social justice has never been greater. The issues are complex. How should social workers view personalisation, for example? In an era of austerity, can social work be about more than simply safeguarding and rationing scarce services? Will the integration of services in areas such as mental health lead to improved services or simply greater domination of medical models? Do social work practices offer an escape from managerialism and bureaucracy or are they simply a Trojan horse for privatisation?

These are some of the questions which contributors to this series – academics, practitioners, service users and movement activists – will address. Not all of those contributing to these texts would align themselves with the critical or radical tradition. What they have in common, however, is a commitment to a view of social work which is much wider than the currently dominant neoliberal models and a belief that notions of human rights and social justice should be at the heart of the social work project.

Poverty and insecurity: Chris Jones and Tony Novak

In this book, Chris Jones and Tony Novak set out to pose, sharply, some fundamental questions about social work within the context of increasingly unequal societies. A number of social scientists have been very good at plotting the growth (and impact) of poverty and inequality in Britain under the impact of neoliberal policy reforms. But what political, moral and social imperatives does this impose on social workers and social work organisations? Social work claims to be an 'ethical career', to be a profession that is value driven, committed to social justice and combatting all manifestations of oppression. Yet faced with the onslaught of austerity, growing inequality and the marketisation of public services – all of which are having a detrimental impact on social work service users and social work practitioners – the social work profession, collectively, has been relatively silent. Jones and Novak's case is that this silence must be broken. Instead, they suggest that if social work is to maintain its claim to be a profession committed to social justice and humanitarianism, then social work organisations and practitioners need to 'speak truth to power' and make clear the horrors being inflicted upon the poorest and most marginalised by state economic priorities.

In their contributions, Mimi Abramovitz, Sanford F. Schram, Suzanne Dudziak and Dimitra-Dora Teloni trace a similar picture of growing inequality and impoverishment of social work services in the US, Canada and Greece. They join the debate and argue for a more 'outspoken' social work that is aware of the iniquities of the modern world and the need for a rejuvenated social work committed to working towards human liberation from poverty and oppression.

"We don't want to be ashamed tomorrow": Poverty, inequality and the challenge to social workers

Chris Jones and Tony Novak

Austere times

We are living in turbulent times. Across the globe, regimes have been toppled and people in unprecedented numbers are taking to the streets in protest as austerity politics sweeps away their jobs and their incomes. The notion that individual debt-fuelled consumerism could provide both the economic drive and the social glue for a rampant capitalism unchallenged in the globe has proved to be disastrous. In the midst of one of the most serious crises of global capitalism, a crisis that is both economic and political, even the most cautious analysts have to face up to the fact that something new is happening in the world. The poor are stirring and rising against their punishment for an economic crisis not of their making; they are angry because the perpetrators are left free and untouched; they are increasingly sickened by the extraordinary disparities in wealth and income; they are insulted by the conspicuous greed and consumption of the rich as their own living standards and well-being decline, and they have had enough of being ignored.

Such stirrings are necessary. Because as well as 'impoverishing the many' capitalism is also plundering the earth's resources with no regard for the human and environmental carnage it brings in its wake. The clock is ticking for the human race. It is a time for clear thinking, strong words and action. It is time for social workers – both academics and practitioners – to speak out and act against the human destruction we are now witnessing.

The scale of hardship that has been dealt out in recent years cannot be underestimated, both nationally and globally. People are hurting and dying now as a result of deepening inequalities and the extraordinarily brutal attack on the most vulnerable which features in virtually all the so-called austerity programmes launched by governments. The current onslaught on the mass of the people everywhere is ferocious, coming, for many in Europe and the US, on top of three decades of neoliberalism, which has eroded living standards and well-being for millions. There is a saying in Greece that you cannot get fat from a fly, but that is not stopping those in power from turning the screw even harder with devastating consequences.

The management of poverty and inequality in the attempt to prevent it from becoming an explosive challenge to the system has for long depended on keeping the gaze of the majority downwards; so that people compare themselves and their fortunes with those beneath them rather than those above. Rarely have people been encouraged to look upwards, and when they did what they saw was justified if not by reference to god-given superiority then by claims of exceptional talent, merit and intelligence. The people's gaze, however, has now shifted considerably upwards, revealing the greed, parsimony and avarice of our elites. Bankers, at one time seen as the paragon of respectability and 'good business sense', are now exposed to all as greedy, ruthless and, what is more, incompetent. People everywhere recoil at the immense amounts of money that are speculated, stolen and wasted to the cost of the jobs and livelihoods of millions, while multinationals sit on vast reserves of capital waiting for wages and conditions to deteriorate further and new 'market opportunities' to arise. And everywhere the politicians who serve this system are regarded with contempt. It is now evident that more and more people have had enough and in diverse places and in diverse ways, some massive and some small, they are on the move. From Egypt to Wall Street, people are demanding justice, an end to inequalities and unsustainable exploitation and, with it, a 'system change'. There is an active international dimension to these struggles that we have not witnessed before, with those in the squares in cities across the globe inspiring one another with their mobilisations, solidarities, initiatives and achievements.

At long last, it seems that more and more people worldwide are making important connections as they search for explanations and strategies for understanding and transforming the grotesque and obscene features of much of our contemporary world. Naming and placing capitalism in the public dock as being the system that has allowed for the simultaneous enrichment of the very few at the cost of poverty to the many is no longer confined to groups on the Left or to those places at the periphery of capitalism where the yoke of exploitation has been most extreme. It is now taking root in the very heartlands of the system itself.

In all its diverse forms what we are witnessing is a global convulsion and movement of the poor. It is notable and united in accurately identifying its core enemy as capitalism, imperialism and the nation states and federations that sustain, manage and legitimise these interconnecting systems. It has brought people together from a wide range of backgrounds and shown the potential for alliance. Sceptics scorn the lack of a systematic programme of action coming from the streets but never highlight the importance and significance of the identification of the enemy. State elites and institutions have invested heavily and systematically in creating divisions between the people with the intent of turning anger and disappointment inwards. They have abused their power and control to construct false enemies and scapegoats to divert attention and dissipate and confuse the majority.[1] How they have delighted as the poor fought each other, white workers against black, Protestants against Catholics, men against women, and left the real cause of their problem unscathed. And yet, despite being deeply embedded and endlessly nurtured, such divisions prove quickly breakable as the sight of Egyptian Christians protecting Egyptian Muslims from the brutality of the state, of migrant and refugee workers being embraced by the social and workers movements of Greece, or of homeless people being embraced by the Occupy protests shows. Such events are profoundly troubling for the status quo.

Huge numbers of people are furious with their political class and its networks and institutions. They feel betrayed and abandoned. Every new revelation that the rich have got richer as the majority move in the opposite direction is like rubbing salt into the wounds. As the gaze deepens and more examples of extraordinary acquisitiveness, greed and embedded corruption emerge so the hypocrisy of the powerful sickens and stimulates resistance.[2] Centuries of effort to seek compliance through divide and rule among the dominated and exploited are now at risk. For many, if not for all, the scales are slipping away and they see so many of the things that have separated them are no more than artifices which weaken as well as divide them.

The British state and 'the problem of the poor'

Of all the industrialised countries, Britain's ruling class has the greatest history in dealing with the problem of poverty and the poor. Fashioned through over five hundred years of uninterrupted capitalist development, its ideas and its policies have sedimented into a particularly callous treatment that marks it off from many of its European neighbours. It is no accident that Britain, one of the richest countries in the world, has levels of poverty and inequality above the European average; it locks up more poor people, spends less on their health and education and has some of the lowest levels of benefit within the European Union.[3] Nor is it accidental that Britain is exceeded in levels of poverty and paucity of state assistance only by the country it helped to form, the United States. Throughout the centuries the rich in Britain have viewed the poor with a disdain that is deeply embedded in their class structure, which asserts their own superiority at the same time as it brands those at the bottom as degenerates, failures, and the like. Their treatment of the poor is also embodied in accompanying ideologies of legitimation which blame, insult and degrade the victim. It is quite simply an outrage and one which over the years has seen some of the most vulnerable (and not so vulnerable) people starved, imprisoned in workhouses, emigrated to the Empire, institutionalised, sterilised, and fast-tracked as inmates of children's homes into prison, joblessness and prostitution.

Ask yourself what words or phrases have been used to describe the poor in Britain: 'the residuum', 'the undeserving', 'the underclass', 'scroungers' are just a few. Now ask yourself how many positive images you can think of. Seeing the poor through such a distorting lens means that they are not heard or seen. They are denied sympathy and understanding. They are punished and seen to deserve even less because it is argued that even pathetically small benefits make them work shy and welfare dependent. As the neoliberal attack has deepened and widened to bring about a massive redistribution of wealth and life chances to the rich and from the poor, engulfing more and more people, so the language of the elites has become more violent and aggressive. 'Scum', 'nasty pieces of work', 'feral underclass' are just some latest examples of the terms used by government leaders to describe some of the poor.[4] They in turn, like John Major at the time of the Bolger tragedy and David Cameron after the British riots in 2011, demand that the time has come to condemn and punish and not make any effort to understand.[5]

An astonishing number of people in Britain go along with such a pathologisation of the poor, even those who themselves are poor by any reasonable standard. As Louise Bamfield, Research Fellow and Secretary to the Fabian Commission on Life Chances and Child Poverty, observed:

> The tendency to blame poverty on deficiencies in personal behaviour is not wholly surprising, given the prevalence of negative stereotypes in the media. But the size of the gap between popular perceptions and the reality of life in poverty is nevertheless profoundly depressing – and difficult territory from which to start to put together a compelling public case for tackling poverty. (Bamfield, 2005)

In the meantime the poorest live in the most extreme conditions of poverty; these include the low-paid, the vast majority of the unemployed, most disabled people, single parents and working-class older people. Many of them have no choice but to depend on the state for survival and do so at the expense of their dignity and freedom. In the face of increasingly whipped-up hysteria about scroungers and benefit cheats, those on disability benefits are being tortured by new eligibility demands and criteria that humiliate, stigmatise and frighten. Young unemployed people are being forced through a variety of mandatory workfare schemes to work in degrading jobs for no return other than their Jobseeker's Allowance (O'Reilly and Clarke, 2011). Funding is evaporating monthly for those dealing with drug and alcohol addictions, HIV, for working-class youth activities and so on, which is wreaking havoc on people's lives and well-being.

But poverty is much more widespread than official statistics suggest. In the middle of this unequal society, and above the very poor, the ordinarily poor struggle to keep their heads above water, to hold on to their jobs and pay the bills. The pressure to consume, which feeds capitalism's relentless search for expansion and markets, does not provide satisfaction but stress. People are not happy. Millions juggle with debts and income to chase a life defined largely by what you possess, and that which is already obsolete and overtaken by some new fashion or invention before you reach it. Compared to the standards set around them, and enjoyed by those at the top, it is scarcely a life of luxury. Most households need two people at work just to get by. For many this means that time with children, family or friends is sacrificed, and the poverty of people's lives increases. The break-up of relationships under stress, violence, abuse, suicide, depression and illness should remind us that poverty is pervasive and cannot be measured in money alone. For the majority the constant haunt that threatens in the background is that through sickness, divorce, unemployment or bad luck they will lose their position and begin an inexorable slide into the ranks of the poorest. So they work harder, and even for less. Most would not count themselves as poor. It would be small wonder if those slightly better off than the poorest did not seek to keep their distance, did not try to avoid being tagged with the same labels and tarred with the same brush. Hostility and resentment towards those dependent on state benefits is not of course the only response, but it is one which plays an important part in weakening solidarity.

Some may also, and this has often been the case, turn their attention downwards and blame those 'below them' – immigrants, welfare dependants – for their situation. In a sense they are right. The competition of the very poor – for work, for housing, for some assistance, even if from the state – impacts on the poor above them, and the mechanisms have long been laid to encourage them to blame each other.

But, however people categorise themselves in terms of class position and poverty, austerity and a major recession are sweeping more and more people into positions where their very capacity to survive has become precarious. Home repossessions are commonplace and households which had previously never been so existentially threatened find themselves homeless. Personal debt has skyrocketed as people have tried to find ways to supplement declining wages from work and/or a much reduced social wage from the state and while facing endlessly rising living costs.[6] Life for a great majority has become a giant, all-enveloping pressure cooker. The notion, for example, that anyone can succeed through dint of living a 'clean' and diligent life, working hard at school and at work is directly contradicted by the experiences of the majority. Any marginal upward social mobility in places such as the US and the UK has evaporated. Notions of living in a meritocracy are now seen as fantasy. As the labour market fosters competition, other areas of state policy work to keep the poor apart. Housing policy commonly segregates the poorest, and in particular those with multiple problems, grouping them in ghettos that confirm their marginality. At the same time, and sometimes from positive motives, initiatives to help one group can foster resentment and animosity from others, scarcely much better off, who remain excluded. Indeed, the state in Britain has often played a skilful hand, knowing when it is necessary to make concessions to some, concessions which often work further to exacerbate divisions and often leave the poorest further behind.

Chopping up the problem and dealing with the fragments has many advantages for the state, not the least by creating a veritable welfare zoo of a plethora of categories which emphasises difference and division at the expense of solidarity in opposition to a system which makes the lives of the poor full of pain and difficulty. Some of it has done damage by focusing on just one aspect of poverty to the neglect of its totality. Who can be just 'fuel poor' or 'water poor' and so forth? And what of 'child poverty' and the distortions which flow from this narrow focus, such as that the children are poor undeservedly because of feckless, irresponsible parents who deserve their poverty. This welfare zoo is well supported by silos of 'poverty' literature that all too often simply don't connect the dots; present shopping lists of reforms that at best are ameliorative and more often useless; and pitifully rarely engage in what New Labour once called 'joined-up thinking'.

In the present crisis the isolation and mistreatment of the poorest is harder to maintain, just as it results in even harsher measures in the attempt to do so. At the same time the justifications for inequality, and in particular the excesses of the rich, appear to be losing their hold. The widespread anger about the greed and economic incompetence of the ruling classes, and the popular support for movements for justice and dignity, suggest a significant shift. The opportunity to widen opposition and to create a common cause across a much greater spectrum of the population is opening up.

Poverty and capitalism

The growing understanding and recognition that poverty is as much a consequence of capitalism as the concentration of power and wealth in the hands of the few has devastating consequences for the legitimacy of the capitalist project. It offers a crucial means of looking at the world that makes increasing sense to people. It explains the mess and who and what is responsible. It identifies corporate greed and companies' extraordinary power; it identifies the state as being for 'the 1%' and not for 'the 99%'.[7] We hope that the depressive voices of post-modernity glorifying in our fragmented identities will now wither away, as they should. Instead there is a growing realisation that only the solidarities of the 99% will bring about justice, dignity and equality and, not least, have any chance of securing a future for the human race on this grossly abused and exploited planet. Consequently, establishing the link between capitalism, inequality and poverty and making it part of our common sense is, in this context, incredibly important. Some may argue that it is only neoliberal, unfettered capitalism that is the problem and not capitalism itself, which can be managed so as to work more responsibly and more equitably. But we've been there before, and look where it got us. Capitalism by its very nature cannot be equitable – competition, exploitation of nature and human labour, private property and profit are all part of its essence. Capitalism creates poverty by its very existence and depends on it for its continuation and can never, ever be part of the solution. Hence, we need to be ready for these apologists who in times past offered crumbs from the table when compelled to but were all too ready to take them back when circumstances allowed.

Embedding the linkage and seeing poverty as a consequence of a particular socio-economic system and not as a personal failure has any number of important consequences. It should at the very least halt the cruel blaming of the victims for their poverty. It should stop us from seeing poverty and the poor as something apart – different and deficient. To date one of the limiting features of otherwise progressive movements has been their neglect of the interests of the poorest. In large part, of course, this is a matter of class. The women's movement of the past half-century has had a huge impact on women worldwide, but the achievement by middle-class women of near-economic equality with men has for many come with the neglect, and even at the expense, of their working-class 'sisters'. From the perspective of 'race', the situation is more complicated. Since people of colour make up the majority of the world's poor, both within and among nations, combating racism has necessarily meant more attention to the poor, but even then huge and growing inequalities among people of colour remain. Other movements too need to take stock; attempts to 'control' pollution by pushing up prices or seeing the threat to the earth's future

–

9

as caused by the numbers of poor people forced (unnecessarily) into semi-existence, not only mistake the enemy and punish the victim, but fail to see the potential that our present organisation of the economy denies. Even within the working class, the poorest have often been left behind. What is now clear is that this has to change. The poorest not only demand it, but without them the struggles of others will be undermined. What, perhaps, various groups are coming to realise is that we all face a common enemy, and that enemy is capitalism. There can be no ecology so long as the rapacious pursuit of profit is the determining factor of economic life, and there is little time left to avert this.

The struggle of the poor and the unfolding dynamics of poverty and inequality will continue to play out with or without the involvement of social workers. But social workers and others involved in welfare provision have an opportunity to cross the barricades and contribute more purposefully to this movement. Surely, as social workers, we no longer need to be convinced that poverty is one of the grossest outrages facing people. Surely, we don't need to be told that poverty is as corrosive of well-being as the strongest acid; of the myriad ways it distorts and diminishes and that any escape from it is largely a matter of luck. We know better than most that its toll on lives far exceeds all other causes combined: that it is poverty which condemns the majority of the human race to vulnerabilities that will never be experienced by those in the gated, gilded and guarded 'communities'.

The poverty literature is immense. Never before have we had access to such a range of material that looks at the manner in which capitalist states and societies have responded to poverty and the poor, although it is also sobering to reflect on the small number of Marxist 'poverty classics' that have been published since Engels' (1845/2009) magisterial *The condition of the English working class*. This should be a core text on every social work course! Engels simply had no truck with those who sought to disguise the destructiveness of urban industrial capitalism as a consequence of the immorality of the working class. The human disasters he encountered in Manchester are victims of a brutal system, and the 'brutish' behaviour of some is, unsurprisingly, one of its consequences.

—

We should have done better within social work to build and develop Engels' work – such as probing his identification of 'anger towards the system' as a critical factor in preventing impoverished individuals and households from collapsing into chaos and self-harm. As Vygotsky demonstrated over a hundred years ago, a revolutionary materialist analysis is the foundation to highly effective therapeutic interventions as he so stunningly revealed in his work with children with learning disabilities and mental health problems (Vygotsky, 1934/1986). It is promising that his work is now attracting the attention of some, especially in education, but the vast majority in social work still remain unaware of this important work.[8]

But in the mass of books and reports on poverty we do now have access to a useful critical literature that has identified the elite prerogatives of ensuring that poverty does not ignite radical political action within the working class, and prevents the persistence of stark inequalities and deep poverty from calling into question the legitimacy of capitalism.[9] These narratives of policy have immense value in highlighting, over time, specific areas of elite concern and anxiety which ought to be included in the mix of influences which shape our strategies. By that we mean that we should focus more on the areas and issues which cause the ruling classes the most concern. And if there is but one lesson that we can learn from a critical reading of British welfare history it is that the legitimation of inequalities and the management of the poor has been a major pre-occupation of the British state. It is a critical arena of class struggle and one in which we must be engaged in the same deliberate and focused way as those who seek to sustain their power.

Speak truth to power

At the very least, the time has come for welfare activists in every arena to use *strong words* to describe the human tragedies which we witness. We don't need to exaggerate. We should recognise that the human stories we must tell can have much greater power to influence than statistics and data. In Greece teachers' reports of children in their class fainting from hunger in suburban Athens had wide media coverage and brought home some of the agonies of the crisis. We distort the reality when we turn away from the effort to describe things as they are and seek refuge in managerial talk and professional and academic gibberish. This country's treatment of its poorest has been brutal and cruel. It remains so, and we should say so. We have more than enough compelling evidence already.

We also need to demand that it is the responsibility of us all to speak out when we see people suffer and be punished without cause or reason. We might be persecuted for it in some cases, but silence can no longer be an alternative. The reasons were set out lucidly by state electricity workers in Greece in November 2011 when they explained why they would refuse to disconnect power supplies to people who could not pay the new austerity tax imposed by the government and now collected through an addition to the electricity bill:

> We are here because those who voted in this despicable law did not even bother to think "but how will the unemployed possibly pay? Will we also cut off their electricity?"
>
> We are here because we refuse to become inhuman murderers of small children and of the sick.
>
> We are here because for us no co-human of ours is in abundance.
>
> We are here because there is still blood running through our veins.
>
> We are here, because humans and their needs are above the markets.
>
> We are here to blockade the disconnection orders for the public good of electricity, without which lives are endangered and no one can live.
>
> Finally, we are here because we do not want to be ashamed tomorrow.
>
> We will not throw our pride and dignity down the drain. (Statement from Greek electricity union, GENOP-DEI, 20 November 2011, published by Indymedia Athens,

https://athens.indymedia.org/front.php3?lang=en&article_
id=1356030, accessed 26 November 2011)

What a testimony to the electricity workers of Greece it would be if social workers adopted a similar statement in organisations such as the Social Work Action Network, workplaces or unions. Its humanity and solidarity is expressed in every line and not least in the recognition that to be compliant would also be a defeat for them: 'We don't want to be ashamed tomorrow. We will not throw our pride and dignity down the drain!'

A key challenge for activists is to ensure that anger and a thirst for fundamental change is not overwhelmed by fear and anxiety as living conditions for the many continue to deteriorate. The widespread attack on people's well-being and security is taking and will continue to take a toll on people's capacity to resist. Furthermore, it is evident that the state, both in the UK and elsewhere, is set on turning the authoritarian screw when it comes to taking on protest and street mobilisations. Police forces everywhere are tooling up with new sprays, gases, water cannon, and tasers, as well as implementing new aggressive methods of crowd control. Then there is the ever-growing resort to the use of prison and the incarceration of increasing numbers of the poor and marginalised. All this is on top of the staggering expansion of state powers to watch and control its own people following 9/11 and the so-called 'war on terror'. Our strategies need to recognise these pressures and our organisations and structures have to face these challenges.[10]

Of course social workers are not going to stop the tide of these kinds of state initiatives, but we can at least make it all the harder. We should no longer accept any suffering in silence; we need to be issuing casualty lists of those wounded and killed by poverty: these terms are much more accurate for reporting on what is, in essence, class warfare; we need to expose the suffering that is hidden from view and the webs of control that the poor have to navigate daily in order to survive. Social workers and countless others employed in the welfare business have access to any amount of material and evidence that illustrates the human costs of current policies. We need to be broadcasting this material. We should be bombarding sympathetic journalists with details of how the austerity measures are currently destroying the lives of some of the most vulnerable in our midst. Social workers in all their various guises and agencies are overwhelmingly preoccupied with the most vulnerable and marginalised. They have a front seat and many of their agencies sadly are implicated in the ongoing massacre of the innocents taking place in the name of deficit reduction.

But where are the howls of anguish derived from that basic human feeling that harm to one is an injury to us all? And where are the howls coming from social work? Where are the floods of letters and calls hitting the local media from outraged social workers who are eyewitnesses to the suffering of the poorest? Where are their voices on the progressive blogs and networks which are now flourishing like never before? When are the so called movers and shakers in the occupation – the directors of social service departments, managers of the big voluntary agencies, professors of social work and the like – going to be hounded for their silence as they scrabble around for the crumbs from the table of the powerful?

Is the absence of a social work howl simply a reflection of an occupation which, like its clients, can be ignored with impunity? In part, yes. Needless to say, those in positions of power and influence within social work don't like to admit to this reality. Yet many social work practitioners at the frontline readily acknowledge this relationship of powerlessness between themselves and their clients, and the correlation between the tabloids' demonisation of the poor and themselves as social workers. They also know only too well that if social work was reserved only for the rich and the privileged, its social standing and influence would be transformed. But ask a client or any person living in an impoverished neighbourhood whether social workers have power and the answer will be an assured 'yes'. We may not have as much power as we would hope for, but powerless, never!

No matter how exhausted and demoralised the social work profession the lack of a sustained 'social work howl' at this point in time is worrying. It cannot be put down to simply 'not knowing'. Nor is it a matter of attitudes or prejudices or evidence that suggests that

—

most social workers have chosen the side of the state as against the side of the client. One of the more significant findings coming out of the interviews we did with front-line social work practitioners in the north of England over a decade ago was the extent of their unanimity over the plight of their clients (Jones, 2001). We came across no social worker who thought that their clients were in any way responsible for their plight; instead, front-line workers talked of working in neighbourhoods that had been ghettoised and suffered years of abandonment, of welfare systems that were wholly inadequate and often cruel, and of poor households who more often than not amazed them by their resilience and initiative rather than shocked them through their behaviour. If we had wanted a critique of the existing welfare system at that time, we could not have wished for a more comprehensive account than that provided by these workers.[11]

There is more than a tinge of self-pity prevalent in British social work which infects social workers across the spectrum of political beliefs. It is not difficult to see why when the occupation has been restructured so many times it seems to be perpetually in the midst of change and confusion; social workers have endured public slander in the media and from successive politicians, and have been decried as sentimentalists with no morality. They have no significant professional representation and often feel unrepresented within the large local government trade unions. Other welfare and health professions are often seen as a threat to social work and are not considered to be firm allies. Those in any sort of leadership position within British social work are ineffective and have no public profile. And the list goes on. All of these factors enfeeble social work and sap energy. Yet in any final reckoning on its contribution to fighting poverty and misery based on the evidence to date, British social work would be condemned for its stupor, lack of integrity and cowardice. These are strong words of condemnation for an occupation which sees itself as positive and progressive but the evidence is compelling.

If anyone wants social work to be part of the future then these tendencies to self-pity and defeatism need to be dismissed. British social workers need to show, in the words of the Greek power workers, that they have 'blood in their veins' and will no longer be shamed by their compliance with the intolerable and the unacceptable. Hence, we need to dispel any notion that what we can do as social workers doesn't matter and won't count. We should act on our analyses to inform our actions. In the case of social work this might include, for example, recognising that sections of the ruling elites have long been preoccupied with ensuring that those who have the closest contacts with the poorest do not, in the language of colonialism, 'go native'. This enduring sensitivity about the reliability and loyalty of state social workers and others has been evident in any number of developments over the past hundred years, not the least in the creation and expansion of professional education across a wide spectrum of state occupations from teachers to social workers. As Max Weber pointed out over a century ago, don't be fooled into thinking that the creation of professional education was simply the result of a newly acquired thirst for knowledge and skills (see Chapter 5, 'The centrality of the social worker' in Jones, 1983). The professional education of teachers and social workers can be much better understood when it is recognised that it is fundamentally concerned with the formation of an expertise socialised to work for the state and not against it.

The state was therefore appalled to see social workers taking to barricades *with* the squatters, as they did in the 1970s, or marching on anti-cuts campaigns *with* service users and allowing their agency photocopiers, phones and duplicators to be used for tenant and community campaigns. We should not underestimate this fear within the ruling elites. Securing the loyalty of the clerks has been a long standing issue for the state. We need to recognise this and act on it.

As state organisationshave their rule books and contracts to manage us and protect themselves, we must have our own tools and organisations to enhance our effectiveness both in defence and in attack. Individual 'kamikaze' social workers will get nowhere fast. We can be certain that actions and resistance from social workers will be met with a counter-attack by agencies and employers. Hence, we must prepare to reduce our vulnerabilities. At this point, it is usual to invoke trade unions as one such tool. Yet for many activists, the trade unions remain a problem. The failure of the trade union bureaucracy to support vigorously the Liverpool social workers' strike in 2004/05, which was about the need to do something about appalling services being offered to clients, is just one case in point. Too many activists have been abandoned by their unions in recent years to allow an unconditional endorsement of trade unions. Some unions are clearly shifting their position and re-evaluating their relationship with the Labour Party, as well as joining in with action on the street, for example during the recent student-led fees demonstrations, and this needs to be pushed further. They could and should play a big role. In the meantime there are progressive groupings across a wide spectrum of health and social services that deeply oppose the onslaught on the poor, such as the Social Work Action Network, In Defence of Youth Work,[12] as well as countless cuts campaigns and service user activist groups. But all these need support, resources and engagement if they are to be effective.

Listening to the movements

In addition to speaking out we must become even more active in supporting and encouraging all service users movements and groups that give voice to their experiences and which promulgate their own proposals for change. Such groups have unparalleled insights and understandings of their challenges and difficulties and the ways to meet them. If they were given control of their services immediately what would emerge would be far superior to anything on offer today. But of course, they have never been given a meaningful opportunity to influence and shape state social policies which affect their lives.

The resourcefulness of the poor is a much neglected contribution to the struggle. We should celebrate what is being achieved and created in the recent eruptions from the street. These are movements of poor people who have to confront and manage their daily survival as well as all their other activities. In the process new forms of mutual aid and solidarities are being created on the ground.[13] Within the tented communities that have been created across the globe progressive health and welfare workers are developing new forms of street

---

practice as they help people deal with the traumas of poverty and hardship. Free of bureaucracy, managerialism and professional elitism we are seeing the outlines of health and welfare services that are compassionate, thoughtful, effective and democratic, and popular.[14] These developments can take time. When people listen to one another with respect, and encourage the widest possible debate, why should we expect detailed programmes to emerge according to time frames that have nothing to do with democracy? As the *indignados* say in Spain: "We are going slowly, because we are going far."

The extent to which the poor have been silenced and barred from influencing policy is extraordinary. Perhaps this is why nearly all state poverty initiatives to date have been spectacularly unsuccessful – just as one would have anticipated given the beast that churns out poverty has not been touched! Ask the working-class poor of Liverpool, for example, what has been the impact of successive national and EU anti-poverty initiatives brought to the city, and the answer is nothing, but most will tell you that their situation today is more dire than ever.

It is no accident that the voices and experiences of the poor are silenced and hidden from view. It is demanded by the imperative of their demonisation. You can't on the one hand insist that the poor are different and deficient and then say let's listen to them and act on what they say. How many children have been abused in children's homes, for example, who were ignored, despite complaining, because as children of some of the poorest in the land, their suffering was belittled, ignored and dismissed?

Poverty and inequality in all its current obscene forms will endure as long as capitalism. Its demise *and* its replacement by a socio-economic system that takes the welfare of the human species as its fundamental principle is the ultimate goal. But in this revolutionary process we need also to develop immediate measures and plans to mitigate the outrages of poverty. And when we listen to the poor, two immediate demands of equal importance emerge. The first is to increase their money income and the other is to change the way they are treated. At the moment, state services and resources to the poor are based on the assumption that the poor can never be trusted, that they will cheat if given half

—

18

a chance and that they will never be able to use extra resources to good effect without supervision. The result is that such services are dehumanising, degrading and despised. They bring shame to all those dependent on the system whether as workers or as recipients.[15]

We won't necessarily get far very quickly if we focus only on changing attitudes and ideas about poverty and the poor. That is why we must insist on immediate ameliorative demands that embody fundamental truths about humanity, dignity, respect and fairness. It is imperative that more money is put into the pockets of the poor. This has been done recently, most commonly in Latin America (Brazil, Venezuela, Bolivia and Argentina, for example), with impressive and immediate results, largely because of the fundamental economic truth that the poor spend their money – unlike the rich and comfortable. It takes no genius to tell us the economic implications in terms of growth and jobs that result from such spending.[16] More money on a secure and long-term basis must be an immediate demand in any serious strategy to reduce the impact of poverty. It is also an entirely self-evident demand, despite the endlessly repeated credo that money to the poor is nearly always wasted money unless carefully supervised. Moreover, it is a strategy that inevitably embraces issues of concern to the vast majority including redistribution, fairness and transparency.

Secondly we should act on the majority's demand for respect and dignity. The entire degrading and humiliating edifice of the state welfare system with its means tests and abuse of household privacy needs to be eradicated. It is only like this because the ruling elites fear and hate the poor. But the demand for respect goes far beyond humanising public welfare provision to encompass the entire world of waged work. Vast swathes of jobs and occupations have disappeared to be replaced by work that for the majority is mind-blowingly unfulfilling. Yes, it is also often casualised, highly exploited, low paid and hazardous, but above all it is mindless and degrading. This is what corrodes our spirits the most. What world would we win by having full employment if this is what would await us?

More and more people are seeing the madness of a world that has shattered humanity by allowing excessive abundance and power for the few at the expense of the many. A planet that can feed and meet the basic needs of every person but allows dealers grow rich in trading and speculating on core foodstuffs leading to hunger and starvation is unsustainable and immoral. Any number of examples can be found to illustrate the madness, not the least the tendency of the rich and the powerful to fence off virtually every aspect of their lives in what Mike Davis (2007) called their 'evil paradises' of gated communities, fenced-off and guarded exclusive shopping areas, six-star hotels, gyms, resorts and who knows what.[17] And they talk about the socially excluded. If we were serious about the concept it is obvious where its application is most appropriate – the minority who control the destiny of so many.

It is a madness that is leading unprecedented numbers of people to take to the streets to search out new ways to re-order the world. It also leading to more people turning to extreme forms of belief whether based in religion or fascism. The impulses are similar in that they feed off a world going mad. Social work for all its imperfections and contradictions has never drawn from these sources. Its statements, if not always its actions, suggest that it stands for something positive. Certainly, there is much in its history to suggest that social workers (but not their agencies) can be part of the solution and not the problem. Wouldn't it be wonderful if we could make it into something that we 'will never be ashamed of tomorrow'?

Notes

[1] Joe Bageant's (2008) book *Deer hunting with Jesus* is crucial reading in that he provides a compelling account of how, among other onslaughts on the white US working class, they have been systematically dumbed down – through schools, media, abandonment and so on – and conned into believing utter rubbish. It is a wonderful detailed insider account of what has happened to his friends and class. However, the rumbles of sheer rage that are now rippling throughout the US as austerity sweeps tens of thousands into homelessness, unemployment and severe poverty are in no small part due to a deep sense of grievance that they have been duped and betrayed.

[2] In an interesting shift, British tabloid newspapers now carry the occasional story detailing the greed of the rich such as that in the *London Standard* on 12 December 2011 which told of a banker's night out at a London club costing him $70,000. It seems in the past his bills were no more than $40,000 for a night out. The explosive public response in 2010 to the widespread rip-off of public money by hundreds of British parliamentarians is indicative of the mood change, not the least towards the blatant hypocrisy of the elites who thieve with almost total impunity whilst the majority are punished and decried for the slightest infraction. Similar emotions were evident in the aftermath of the summer riots of 2011 in various parts of London and other major English cities. Russell Brand's comments won him much support when he wrote: 'Why am I surprised that these young people behave destructively, "mindlessly", motivated only by self-interest? How should we describe the actions of the city bankers that brought our economy to its knees in 2010? Altruistic? Mindful? Kind? But then again, they do wear suits, so they deserve to be bailed out, perhaps that's why not one of them has been imprisoned. And they got away with a lot more than a few fucking pairs of trainers." ('Big Brother isn't Watching You', 11 August 2011, www.russellbrand.tv/2011/08/big-brother-isnt-watching-you/, accessed 3 Jan uary2012).

[3] There is an abundance of data sources for up-to-date figures and comparisons. The following websites are good places to start:

- Breadline Britain (BBC): http://news.bbc.co.uk/1/hi/in_depth/business/2005/breadline_britain/default.stm
- Child Poverty Action Group (CPAG): www.cpag.org.uk/
- Institute of Public Policy Research: www.ippr.org.uk
- Joseph Rowntree Foundation: www.jrf.org.uk/
- And not least the books by Richard Wilkinson who, whilst no revolutionary, has assiduously brought together a range of data to illustrate both the deepening divides between the rich minority and the poor majority and their appalling consequences for individual and societal welfare. See *The impact of inequalities: how to make sick*

societies healthier (Wilkinson, 2005) and *The spirit level: why equality is better for everyone* (Wilkinson and Pickett, 2010).

[4] We go into more detail on the moral condemnation of the poor and the recent drift to deeper abuse in our *Poverty, welfare and the disciplinary state* (Jones, and Novak,1999). Owen Jones has provided a valuable update in *Chavs: The demonization of the working class* (Jones, 2011).

[5] An unprecedented number of young people with no previous convictions have been imprisoned following their arrests even for trivial offences. The police are especially intent on taking their revenge for their loss of control, especially in London, with Scotland Yard maintaining a high profile on its pursuit of all offenders and in publicising details and photographs of those sentenced and those hunted. See, for example, www.bbc.co.uk/news/uk-england-london-16297723 (accessed 3 January 2012) for further details of Scotland Yard's campaign. See also Hallsworth and Brotherton (2011) *Urban disorder and gangs: a critique and a warning* for a valuable and critical discussion of the British riots in August 2011 and the state's misguided and ill-informed responses.

An excellent source on Britain's prison population and prisons is The Prison Reform Trust's *Bromley Briefings Prison Factfile,* December 2011, www.prisonreformtrust.org.uk/Portals/0/Documents/Bromley%20Briefing%20December%202011.pdf, accessed 3 January 2012.

[6] Average household debt in the UK is £7,984 (excluding mortgages). This figure increases to £15,353 if the average is based on the number of households that actually have some form of unsecured loan. Average household debt in the UK is £55,808 (including mortgages). The average owed by every UK adult is £29,539 (including mortgages). This is 122% of average earnings. Other highlights from debt statistics issued by Credit Action in December 2011 include:

- 331 people every day of the year will be declared insolvent or bankrupt. This is equivalent to one person every 60 seconds during a working day.

- Citizens Advice Bureaux dealt with 8,910 new debt problems every working day in England and Wales during the year ending June 2011.
- The average cost of raising a child from birth to the age of 21 is £27.50 a day.
- 101 properties were repossessed every day during the third quarter of 2011.
- 142 new people became unemployed for more than 12 months every day during the 12 months to end September 2011.
- 1,611 people reported they had become redundant every day during the three months to end September 2011
- 193 mortgage possession claims will be issued and 153 mortgage possession orders will be made today.
- 402 landlord possession claims will be issued and 274 landlord possession orders will be made today.

From: 'UK Debt Statistics from Credit Action', December 2011, www. creditaction.org.uk/helpful-resources/debt-statistics.html (accessed 4 January 2012).

[7] There is much we could say about the emergent terms of the 1% and 99%. But whatever the drawbacks, the kernel of truth contained in the slogans concerning the manner in which capitalism in its current form serves the interests of only a small minority makes it a potent cry and one that can be developed and built on.

[8] See the Lev Vygotsky archive in the Marxist Internet Archive at www.marxists.org/archive/vygotsky/.

[9] See for example, Novak (1988); Stedman Jones (1971); Fox Piven and Cloward (1972), Mooney and Lavalette (2000).

[10] Despair is not an option. We are the majority and we have right on our side and we have many examples of how we can sustain ourselves in periods of acute difficulty. And we say this with great seriousness, as long as we can sing, dance, laugh and play together we will prevail!

[11] Sadly not all social workers are like this, but many are. Social work has always been full of contradictions, including its ability to attract the very best and the very worst of people.

---

[12] Below is the last part of an open letter, from the In Defence of Youth Work group, which reflects some of the issues raised in this chapter. The comments on the letter are also worth reading.

> Of course it is easy to spout rhetoric on paper. Doing something solid with this analysis is another matter altogether. This is especially the case, given the very different settings occupied by youth workers today. Without doubt the space to duck and dive, to argue and criticise, varies enormously. Yet this very diversity lends weight to the proposal we would like to make, which is quite simply that we must come together to clarify what is going on in all its manifestations; to understand better how we can support each other in challenging the dire legacy of these neo-liberal years.
>
> If we possess the wit and energy to do so, we will not be alone. (http://www.indefenceofyouthwork.org.uk/wordpress/?page_id=90, accessed 24 November 2011).

[13] We should not underestimate the extent to which these seemingly new initiatives have more often than not been informed and shaped by earlier popular and organic social and community work initiatives that exist almost out of sight in so many poor neighbourhoods across the world.

[14] And it is not just health and welfare. There have been significant educational developments, ranging from public lectures and open debates to creating libraries and universities. Commenting on the Occupy Wall Street (OWS) movement in the US, Jules Lobel made the following observation:

> Perhaps the most critical component of OWS is its creation of alternative communities which reflect the egalitarian, democratic world that its activists seek for the future. Sometimes referred to as 'pre-figurative politics', this perspective seeks to create in microcosm the alternative models that reflect the future world that the activists support, while at the same time using those institutions to engage in direct action to change the

—

current reality. By creating a community dedicated to solidarity, consensus decision-making, everyone's participation, respect for everyone's opinion, and equality, OWS attempted to demonstrate that another world is possible, not in theory but in practice. That effort creates hope for a radically different future, which in many respects is more or equally important than winning particular demands. As Matthias Schwartz pointed out in a recent *New Yorker* article, 'In the end, the point of Occupy Wall Street is not its platform so much as its form, people sit down and hash things out instead of passing their complaints on to Washington.' As the slogan around the encampment went, 'We are our demands.'" (Lobel (2011) 'The Future of the Occupy Movement', *Common Dreams*, 6 December, http://www.commondreams.org/view/2011/12/06-6, accessed 7 December 2011)

[15] It is worth recalling Toni Morrison's comment on how to break the 'cycle of poverty', given that 'you can't just hand out money': "Why not? Everybody [else] gets everything handed to them ... I mean what people take for granted among the middle and upper classes, which is nepotism, the old-boy network. That's the shared bounty of class", cited by Turner (2011).

[16] See Anderson (2011) for an insightful discussion of Lula's strategy with respect to poverty.

[17] It is no great comfort to learn that the more the elites spend on their fences the more insecure they seem. It seems that security addiction is an ever-lurking danger and they can't get enough of devices, gadgets and fortifications that make them feel safe. For excellent details, see Minton (2009).

Which side are we on?

Mimi Abramovitz

'"We don't want to be ashamed tomorrow": poverty, inequality and the challenge to social workers' is a progressive/radical manifesto that challenges social workers to fight back against today's mounting inequality, deepening poverty, and the austerity-driven attack on programmes for the poor and working classes. Jones and Novak, who see social workers as the 'eyewitnesses to the suffering of the poorest' ask us to protest against current conditions with both 'howls of anguish' and active resistance to the effort by business and the state to secure their interests by legitimating inequality, dismantling social welfare programmes, and disciplining the poor.

Social workers sit at the intersection between individuals and the state – where the needs of the state and the individual often clash – a location that may ease or complicate responding to this call. Will we be silenced in the current political climate where siding with progressive social change appears unfashionable, if not risky? The following discussion contextualises the current attack on the public sector, provides a basis for deciding which side we are on and otherwise engages in the political struggle endorsed by Jones and Novak. It identifies: (1) the contradictory functions of US welfare state, (2) the relationship between dismantling the welfare state and the wider neoliberal agenda, and (3) the three-pronged impact of the assault on women and persons of colour as the major public sector programme users, workers, and union members.

—

The regulatory and liberatory functions of the US welfare state

The US welfare state carries out a contradictory set of social, economi, and political functions that both uphold status quo and create the conditions for social change. The *social functions* of the welfare state support the status quo by requiring clients to comply with prevailing work and family norms. However, the programmes also provide access to the social wage (eg non-market income) that can help workers to avoid the low-paid jobs, and women to avoid unhappy or dangerous relationships. The *economic functions* of the welfare state benefit business by lowering labour costs and fuelling consumption, profits and economic growth. However, like a strike fund, access to the social wage can increase the leverage and therefore the bargaining power of workers with employers, and of women at home. *Politically* the welfare state helps the powers-that-be by quelling the discontent produced when market inequality contradicts the democratic promise of equal opportunity for all. However, welfare state benefits also have the potential to shift the balance of power from the haves to the have-nots. In sum, the welfare state regulates the lives of the poor, enhances profits and mutes social unrest. Yet its liberatory possibilities pose a threat to the status quo, turning the welfare state into a site of political struggle for social workers (Abramovitz, 2004).

The neoliberal strategy

By the mid-1970s, the liberatory potential of the welfare state began to threaten its regulatory functions thereby fuelling the elite's effort to rein in 'big government'. The modern welfare state emerged in the 1930s as part of the New Deal established to mediate the impact of the first economic crisis of the 20th century by redistributing income downwards and expanding the role of the state. Fuelled by post-war peace, prosperity and pressure from popular movements, the welfare state expanded until the mid-1970s, when the second economic crisis of the 20th century undercut business profits. The current attack, a response to this ongoing crisis, is best understood as part of the broader neoliberal strategy designed to restore profitability by undoing the New Deal. Designed to redistribute income upwards and downsize the state, the now familiar tactics include: (1) tax cuts and a less progressive tax code, (2) programme retrenchment; (3) privatisation (shifting government services to the private sector); (4) devolution (shifting federal responsibility to the states); and (5) weakening social movements best positioned to fight this austerity plan. At the same time, the Right has called for the restoration of family values and a colour-blind social order (Abramovitz, 2004).

To win public support for measures that undermined personal economic security and the common good, the anti-government forces sealed the deal with the race, 'welfare-queen', gay marriage, and/or immigration cards. The resulting politics of fear and hate have kept people divided, blinded to their shared interests, and – until recently – demobilised. The elite also made calculated use of what Naomi Klein (2007) calls the 'shock doctrine' or the creation and manipulation of crisis to impose policies that people would not otherwise stand for. In the US elected officials created budget crises by refusing to raise taxes while continuing to spend. By 2011 federal revenues had dropped to their lowest level since 1950, while federal spending rose to 25.3% of the GDP in 2011 – the highest level since World War II (due mostly to the costs of Middle East wars and health care) (Merrick and Thorney, 2012). After creating a $1.3 trillion deficit, legislators played to fears of a ballooning debt to press for more cuts to spending but not any tax cuts. They dismissed analyses showing that tax cuts accounted for 50% of the revenue gap from 2001 to 2007, compared to 10% for entitlement and 7% for discretionary spending (Greenstein, 2012); ignored later data showing that the cost of means-tested programmes will not add to long-term fiscal problems (Greenstein, 2012); and rejected the idea the expiration of the Bush tax cuts would halve the deficit by 2021 (Center on Budget and Policy Priorities, nd). Discounting these data and evoking the shock doctrine, government foes targeted the popular entitlement programmes – once regarded as the 'third rail' of politics. The recently proposed Ryan (R-WI) budget goes further, with a long-term spending path designed to dismantle most of the federal government by 2050 (except for social security, health care, and defence). Unlikely to pass Congress intact, it nonetheless promises to set the agenda for months to come. Washington's budget cuts translate into less federal aid to states that have created their own budget crises by failing to raise taxes. They too evoke the shock doctrine to win support for spending $75 billion less in 2012 than in 2011.

The war on the welfare state is a war on women

The neoliberal effort to dismantle the welfare state falls heaviest on women, who comprise the majority of public sector programme *users* but also its *employees* and *union members*, and on persons of colour, who are over-represented in all three groups. The conservative agenda has targeted these groups since the 1980s with little impunity. Indeed, it was not until women became identified as a swing vote during the 2012 presidential campaign that the 'war on women' made headline news.

Welfare state programme users lose services

The first prong of the 'war on women' targeted women as *users* of services that specifically address their needs, such as reproductive health services (Guttmacher Institute, 2012), affordable health care, protection against entrenched sex-based wage discrimination and violence against women,[1] as well as the Women, Infants, and Children (WIC) nutrition programme (US Department of Agriculture, Food and Nutrition Service, 2011) and maternal and child health services (National Women's Law Center, 2011). However, women also lose out when other programmes end up on the chopping block, such as the nation's major entitlement programmes including social security (57% female), Medicare (56% female) and Medicaid (54% female) (Campbell, 2011), as well as $1.2 trillion in reduced spending over the next decade for Head Start, K-12 education, job training, Pell Grants, housing and many other essential programmes.[2] Given that women still have near-exclusive responsibility for the home, these programmes critically ease the tension that arises when the requirements of profitable production

---

(low wages, high unemployment, and so on) fail to provide families with the standard of living needed to maintain themselves and sustain the future workforce. The programmes also help women to balance work and family responsibilities; provide families with a modicum of income, health and education; and reduce barriers to job, educational and other opportunities. In brief, when officialdom cuts welfare state programmes that subsidise the costs and responsibility of women's socially prescribed care work, the loss shifts the burden of family maintenance back to women's unpaid labour in the home.

Fewer public sector jobs for women

Welfare state employment historically operated as an important route of upward mobility for women and persons of colour whom the private sector excluded (Abramovitz, 2004). The New Deal opened public sector jobs to women and persons of colour beginning in the 1930s. These workers also benefited from the post-World War II expansion of the welfarism driven in part by victories of the labour, civil rights and women's movements. By January 2011 women comprised 57% of all government workers: 43% of federal, 51% of state and 61% of local government (National Women's Law Center, 2011b; Feinstein, 2011). The public sector also became the single most important employer for blacks, who are more likely than other workers to hold public sector jobs (Ali et al, 2011). More than 14% of all public sector workers are black compared to most other sectors where they comprise only 10% of the workforce (Pitts, 2011).

The 2007 economic meltdown, the ensuing recession and the neoliberal attack on 'big government' cost the nation many public sector jobs. Men initially suffered most of the job losses because construction and other 'male' jobs go first during most downturns. However, the recovery has been tougher on women who lost 70% of the 573,000 public sector jobs that disappeared between June 2009 and March 2012 (National Women's Law Center, 2012) – due mostly to tax cuts in the red (Republican) states.[3] Women gained only 12.3% of 2.3 million net jobs added to the overall economy. Proposed spending cuts will cost the economy 4.1 million government jobs through 2014 (Pollock, 2012).

Loss of union rights

The neoliberal strategy also weakened the influence of the labour movement, best positioned to resist the austerity programme. Total union membership fell from a peak of 35% of the civilian labour force (1954) to 11.8% (2011) – the lowest percentage of union workers since the Great Depression. Compounded by deindustrialisation and globalisation, private sector unionisation fell to 6.9% in 2010 and 2011 (US Department of Labor, Bureau of Labor Statistics, 2011). With 93% of private sector workers lacking union protection, corporate America won the day. However public unions withstood the onslaught, holding their average membership at more than 37% (Aronowitz, 2011). Seeking to finish the job, the opponents of labour and 'big government' turned against the labour movement's last stronghold, the public sector. Given that 61% of unionised women but only 38% of unionised men work in the public sector, the attack added a third prong to the attack on women who also suffered as programme users and workers (Laborers' International Union of North America, 2011). Governors demonised government employees as the new privileged elite (calling them *lazy* and *overpaid*), defined collective bargaining rights rather than tax cuts as the enemy of a balanced budget, stripped teachers and nurses of their labour rights while sparing the male-dominated police and firefighters unions. The loss of union protection will set women back. Trade union women of all races in both public- and private-sector jobs earn nearly one third more a week than non-unionised women, although white women earn more than women of colour. They suffer a smaller gender wage gap and are more likely than their non-unionised sisters to have employer-provided health insurance and pension plans.

Loss of a strong advocate

Unions are one of the few influential players with the interest and potential to represent the middle and working classes. Public sector unions historically pressed for high-quality services, dependable benefits and fair procedures for themselves and others. In the 1920s, the American Federation of Teachers stood up for greater school funding and smaller class sizes. In the 1960s unionised social workers in the US fought for fair hearings and due process for welfare recipients. In the 1980s and 1990s home care workers sought more sustained care for their clients. Unions provide a check against unmediated corporate power inside and outside government. The loss of union power will cost public sector programme users, workers, *and* union members a strong advocate.

Conclusion

This analysis of the welfare state's contradictory functions, neoliberal retrenchment strategies and the three-pronged attack on women and persons of colour suggests the need for, and possible points of, intervention. In state after state thousands of government workers and supporters have risen up in anger to say that they will not take the assault on their well-being, dignity and rights lying down. Occupy Wall Street's championship of 'the 99%' has made mounting inequality and the need for a more robust public sector front-page news for the first time in many years. A cross-section of social workers have also spoken out. Some people argue that when social work resists oppression it politicises a previously neutral, objective and apolitical profession. Those who take this position forget: (1) that social work has always been political given that it deals with human consciousness or the allocation of resources; (2) that tolerance of state actions that violate professional or humane standards bolsters society's more conservative forces and risks alignment with them; and (3) that by allowing the status quo to stand unchallenged 'neutrality' itself becomes a political stance that favours the haves over the have-nots. Since social workers cannot avoid the political, Jones and Novak argue that it is far better to address these issues explicitly than to pretend that they do not exist. The history of our profession suggests that fighting for social change represents a more ethical option than practising a non-political social work. The middle ground, if one ever existed, is fast receding today. As Jones and Novak indicate, social workers and the social work profession must decide 'whose side we are on'.

Notes

[1] The Guttmacher Institute (2012) reported that in early 2012 legislators in 45 states introduced 944 provisions to limit women's reproductive health and rights including the pre-abortion use of medically unnecessary and physically intrusive sonograms, bans on abortions during the first 8–20 weeks after fertilisation, which flouts the *Roe v Wade* standard of fetal viability; the omission of reasonable exceptions for women's health, rape, incest or grievous fetal impairment, and depriving access to life-saving breast and cervical cancer screening and other preventive health services for thousands of otherwise under-servedlow-income women by defunding Planned Parenthood. Opponents of women's rights have also blocked federal and state laws designed to overcome entrenched sex-based wage discrimination.

[2] www.nwlc.org/resource/ryan-budget-fy-13-gutting-vital-programs-women-and-families-giving-trillions-tax-cuts-milli

[3] 'Austerity is the real threat to women's job growth', available at: http://sbronars.wordpress.com/tag/womens-job-losses/

Neoliberalism and welfare: the Canadian experience

Suzanne Dudziak

Chris Jones and Tony Novak speak eloquently about the expanding inequality and poverty now evident throughout the world and why all of us, especially social workers, should be moved to 'clear thinking, strong words and action'.

I begin this comment by identifying some shared points of analysis and also some differences when comparing neoliberalism in Canada to Britain. In response to Jones and Novak's call to action, I also address the issue of alternatives and the necessity of taking action.

The Canadian context

The story in Canada is remarkably similar with regard to the development and impacts of neoliberal discourse and policy implementation when compared with Britain. The differences that exist are largely due to Canada being a middle power with a much smaller economy and population, and due to our proximity to the US. In the Canadian context, US hegemony, in terms of economic integration and political and cultural influence, cannot be underestimated.

Following Beveridge and Keynes post-World War II, Canada's social safety-net evolved in patchwork fashion and more slowly than in Britain but by 1966, for example, universal health care and social assistance had been achieved, along with significant investments in education and an expanding public sector. These social programmes lasted 30 years before being eroded or dismantled entirely in the mid-1990s by the same federal Liberal Party that had brought them into existence. What remains today are decentralised fragments of social

—

services that vary widely from province to province according to the degree of economic austerity being exercised.

The economic crisis of the early 1980s, subsequent recessions and rising debt and deficits in Canada, which neoliberals used to justify cutting social programmes, were actually manufactured by the Canadian political and business elite. In the Canadian version of Thatcherism and Reaganomics, the Bank of Canada deliberately slowed economic growth with higher interest rates and adopted a policy of high unemployment even though inflation was low (Stanford, 1998, p 42). While this policy of 'permanent recession' led to significant deficits, which favoured the financial sector that serviced government borrowing, allowing 8.5% unemployment as a way to discipline labour costs signalled the end of state investment in job creation and of support for the victims of capitalism (Stanford, 1998, p 42). As Teeple and McBride (2011) state, 'the policies were aimed at shifting the growing working-class share of the total social product back to corporations and the private accumulation process, and were accompanied by the construction of a new set of institutions and practices to replace or modify those aligned with Keynesianism' (p xii). Canada's participation in a Free Trade Agreement with the US in 1988 and in NAFTA with the US and Mexico in 1993 solidified the new hegemony of corporate rights over political rights and democratic institutions. With the loss of 600,000 manufacturing jobs by the year 2000, the shift from industrial production to the export of natural resources led one economist to call Canada 'the largest undeveloped country in the West': unprocessed and semi-processed resource exports now account for two-thirds of Canada's total exports; and high value-added finished products account for just one-third of exports (Campbell, 2012, p 2).

The resultant mass structural unemployment has led to a bottoming-out of the middle class and the creation of a new class of 'the working poor': families who are one pay-cheque away from poverty and who depend on food banks to supplement incomes.[1] With a now 'flexible' labour force, workers are forced to migrate for work in distant mines or oil sands.

Increasing poverty and inequality

Despite claims by the Conservative Government that Canada fared relatively well during the 2008 Great Recession,[2] the gap between those living in poverty and middle and high income earners continues to widen. In addition to the loss of permanent jobs, current unemployment data indicates that the biggest loss of jobs since November 2011, was in part-time and seasonal work, affecting the working poor and women, in primarily the provinces of Atlantic Canada where unemployment is over 10%. At the same time, the federal government has targeted seasonal workers with cuts to employment insurance benefits for repeat users (Georgetti, 2012).

In addition to jobs and housing issues, food insecurity is now a serious problem, affecting at least 10.8% of families with at least one child under 6 years of age.[3] According to Food Banks Canada, 55% of Canadian families whose main source of income is social assistance are food insecure and rely on food banks each month (CCPA, 2012, p 2).

As in Britain the transition from welfare capitalism to neoliberal capitalism is marked by attacks on the poor in discourse as well as policy. Swanson (2001), a Canadian anti-poverty activist, analysed the social construction of 'poor-bashing' sponsored by corporate-backed institutions, think tanks and the media and aimed at denigrating and controlling the disenfranchised and masking rising inequality. 'Poor-bashing' has been used to further undermine social programmes and to justify policies such as workfare and 'snitch-lines' to capture 'welfare cheats'. And as Jones and Novak rightly point out, one of the weaknesses of progressive movements 'has been their neglect of the interests of the poorest' (p 8). This critique has to be directed squarely at social work academics and practitioners for our collective failure as a profession to defend the rights of the poor, whom we claim as our major constituency.

Action and alternatives

The now famous environmental story of the frog placed in water that is gradually heated up until the frog expires reminds me of social work in relation to neoliberalism. Social work knowledge is replaced by standardised computer formulae aimed at the bottom line, social work standards of practice are reduced to lists of competencies and techniques, and social work jobs are eliminated or replaced with less expensive service workers, and the profession says little and does nothing. It seems that to act would be considered 'unprofessional' even when it means our own demise. Thus, some of us 'adjust' to the warming water as is expected of our clients. However, for those of us who are feeling the heat and stress, Jones and Novak suggest some serious reflection '[to establish] the link between capitalism, inequality and poverty and [make] it part of our common sense' and to understand our experience 'as a consequence of a particular socio-economic system and not personal failure' (p 8). In this regard, political and economic literacy, including a structural analysis of neoliberalism, needs to be part of the social work curriculum and continuing education for social workers these days if the 'anti-oppressive practice' we profess is to have any meaning.

For those of us who are ready to get out of the water and to work at turning off the tap, Jones and Novak encourage us to join in common cause with others to organise and resist. Their enthusiasm for the recent Occupy movement is a case in point. I view Occupy as a sign of those feeling the heat starting to react against rather than adjust to life-threatening conditions. Naming the hegemony of the 1% is a hopeful sign in this regard, indicating a class awareness of who's keeping the tap turned on and why. And it seems to be having some positive impact in terms of supporting alternatives. For example, a recent Canadian poll indicates that the 75% of Canadians think that the inequality gap is a serious problem with long-term consequences, and the majority are willing to pay higher taxes to support social programmes as well as calling for higher taxes for the 1% (*Toronto Star*, 2012). Challenging the dominant discourse is a beginning. In countries

—

like Canada, where the history of class struggle is weaker than in the UK, the exception being Quebec,[4] the current street resistance in the European Union to neoliberal austerity regimes helps to legitimate the democratic right to protest for many who have never done so. At the same time, it also demonstrates the necessity for strategies that can facilitate prolonged organised resistance and which operate at local, national and transnational levels, if actual structural change in social and economic conditions is to occur.

The good news is that many social movements today are challenging capitalism and making the links across sectors and transnationally in solidarity with one another.[5] As Jones and Novak point out, in social work the creation of Social Work Action Networks (SWANs) in some advanced capitalist societies means that we now have a vehicle for sharing information, doing analysis and organising resistance in common cause with our colleagues in the Global South to defend the rights of working people and the poor. Ultimately, this is the 'social work' our future depends on.

Notes

[1] Similar to Jones and Novak's analysis in calling for dignity and respect 'in the entire world of waged work', the term 'working poor' in the Canadian context refers to the bifurcated restructuring of work in Canada consisting of precarious, poorly paid, part-time jobs at one end and a few highly paid niche jobs at the other end. From 2000 to 2008, numbers of those working at the minimum wage level increased by 750,000. In 2008, 35% of all jobs were non-standard: part-time, temporary, contract or self-employed (Langille, 2010).

[2] Regarding the 2008 global financial meltdown and claims by Prime Minister Stephen Harper that Canada had the soundest banking system in the world, not requiring bailouts, economist David Macdonald uncovered data that indicates 'Canada's banks were the recipients of $114 billion in support from the Bank of Canada, the US Federal Reserve, and the Canada Mortgage and Housing Corporation (CMHC)'(Macdonald, 2012, p 1).

[3] According to a report by Olivier De Schutter, Special Rapporteur on the Right to Food, 'A growing number of people across Canada remain unable to meet their basic food needs. In 2007/2008, approximately 7.7% of households in Canada reported experiencing moderate or severe food insecurity. Approximately 1,920,000 people in Canada, aged 12 or older, lived in food insecure households, and a staggering one in 10 families – 10.8% – with at least one child under the age of 6 were food insecure during the same period' (CCPA, 2012, p 2).

[4] Quebec has a long and unique history in Canada of organised militant labour unions and parties of the Left. Strong social movements have resulted in substantial gains in terms of social welfare. The student movement is one example. In response to a neoliberal proposal to raise tuition fees in early 2012, 200,000 college and university students took to the streets in what became the longest student strike in North America. The movement helped to defeat the Liberal Party in a recent provincial election.

[5] While Jones and Novak's critique of white, liberal, middle-class feminists is justified, it must also be noted that the women's movement was one of the first to challenge poverty and inequality as impacts of globalisation. The World March of Women began in Quebec in 1995, became Canada-wide in 1996 and grew into a global action in 2000 involving over 150 countries (Rebick, 2005, p 246).

Social work and the Greek crisis

Dimitra-Dora Teloni

The following comments will not be neutral not only because the insightful work of the authors – concerning poverty, social policy and social work – has been for years a source of inspiration for me but mainly because this text was written in May 2012 in Greece, where I live and work. More specifically, two years after the entrance of the International Monetary Fund (IMF) and Central Bank with the alliance of Greek elite, the people are getting poorer and poorer day after day. The unemployment rate has risen to 25%,[1] while there are constant cuts in salaries and pensions as well as the abolition of benefits. The statistics demonstrate an increase of up to 20% in suicides over the last two years alone. Similarly, the incidence of depression, drug use and mental health problems has increased significantly. Poverty, as Jones and Novak highlight, is not only about the lack of money; it is much more and its effects on people's lives are more than apparent in austerity Greece.

Faced with such human tragedy you cannot be neutral. This is particularly true for social work. The commitment of social work to social justice and the well-being of people is a clear indication of which side social work should be on. Jones and Novak make a clear call to social workers to use 'strong words' and take action against the human destruction.

However, critical analysis of the general context is a basic precondition before taking action. At this point, the authors describe vividly the situation across the globe and contribute to providing the reader with an insightful understanding.

The following comments focus on two points of the authors' analysis. The first point that will be discussed is the management of poverty

---

under capitalism and the tactics of the system, using examples from the Greek case. The second point refers to the resistance of the people and the need for social work to take action.

To begin with the first point, the authors highlight how poverty and inequality are clearly connected with capitalism. Capitalism has systematically used a number of 'tools' in order to keep its dominance through the management of poverty. The authors describe how the management of poverty 'prevent[s] it from becoming an explosive challenge to the system'. In other words, through a variety of tactics, the elites attempt to keep the poor silent. Therefore, the system leads people 'to compare themselves … with those beneath them rather than those above'. This is a significant point of how people are taught to think.

Another significant point is the concept of 'blaming the victim' (meaning the poor). To my mind, the concept of the poor as being to blame for their poverty is not only used with regard to the poor as individuals living in a specific country but with regard to the poor as a specific group of people living around the world and being responsible for the economic crisis the world is facing today. For example, over the last two years Greece has been traduced across Europe, and Greek people have been labelled as lazy and corrupt. It is now a country that has to be punished by the IMF and the Central Bank. Once again, it is the people who are responsible for paying for a crisis that they didn't create. A whole country is punished so that the message will be spread all over Europe. Countries like Greece are not only used as 'scapegoats' for the crisis but also as the guinea pigs of Europe in the elites' attempt to increase the profits of the bankers.

Additionally, as Jones and Novak describe, the 'divide and rule' tactic is used in order to ensure the profit of the elites. Thus, in Greece, for example, they attempted systemically (and mainly through the media) to turn one class against another. For about a decade, the concept of the 'lazy' public servant has been successfully used by the media and politicians in order to minimise the public sector and promote privatisation (such as in health sector, the railways, electricity and so on). However, the attempts at privatisation have met with obstacles due to the resistance of the workers. At this point, the next move was

—

threats against people and the spread of fear. National elites within the EU and later the IMF and the Central Bank, with the co-operation of the media, systematically threaten the Greeks. The dilemma has been clearly set: we either abide by our obligations or we will be led to disaster. However, these obligations refer to the most extreme austerity policies, which unsurprisingly have led to disaster: the ruination of the lives of the people, which is an obvious fact since the pauperisation of the population is massive.

Clearly, capitalism finds different ways to establish its dominance. As Jones and Novak describe, if propaganda does not work any more, fear and threatening take its place. Fear can be successfully used in propaganda but if this doesn't seem to work effectively, then it's time to use other tactics particularly in order to successfully handle those who keep resisting. In the Greek case physical violence was often used by the police against the demonstrators and the massive gatherings of people in Syntagma Square in the summer of 2011. Brutality, tear gas and attacks against people are the ultimate means used by the state to terrify and disperse demonstrators and push them back to their houses.

Nevertheless, as Jones and Novak describe, something new is happening across the globe: the ongoing increase in the number of the poor who cannot stand paying for the crisis that they didn't create any longer. The authors refer to the movements in squares across the world and the massive demonstrations as a sign that something is changing. Contrary to Jones and Novak, many attempted to understand the squares' movement through a simplistic way of thinking. For example, in Greece, some left-wing analysts criticised this movement for incorporating both nationalists and those on the Left or for not having a clear political strategy and task. Undoubtedly, some of these criticisms need to be borne in mind. However, social phenomena should be analysed after a certain period of time has gone by and not seen as snapshots in history's evolution. In the Greek case, the squares' movement was an opportunity for people to try other new (old) ways of acting democratically. For many people, it was the first time they had come out on the streets, shared with others their anger and despair, talked openly and taken decisions in democratic open grassroots assemblies. These actions are new experiences for people and in any case, as Jones and Novak describe, the new growing movement on the streets across the globe has identified the same 'enemy'. Moreover, to my mind, these initiatives which are characterised by solidarity are signs that we are trying out in practice new forms of exchanging ideas, discussing in public but mainly attempting new forms of grassroots action.

The squares' movement in Greece like other neighbourhood initiatives of the people are important. For example, in many neighbourhoods across Greece, citizens have created networks of solidarity for the unemployed: they exchange products and organise common meals. Additionally, health professionals, particularly in the big cities, create grassroots structures such as provision of medical care for the poor (for both Greeks and immigrants), and for children, and they organise common meals, and so on.

It is possible to find some social workers involved in these initiatives here and there. However, social workers do not connect their everyday work with the resistance of the people in neighbourhoods. This is not a surprise. The silence of official social work is deafening. It keeps its silence not only about the poverty and suffering of the people. It is also silent whenever the system creates 'scapegoats' such as immigrants,[2] people suffering from HIV,[3] and so on. In this silence, Greek Social Work Action Network is an exception; however, there is a lot to be done.[4]

On the other hand, in the Greek context, welfare provision and services have been minimised more than ever. Consequently, front-line social workers have no means to help their clients, whose numbers have dramatically increased. I often listen to practitioners describing how the profile of the users has rapidly changed. It is no longer the excluded, stigmatised, 'problematic' families and the 'lazy' poor who need social services. It is now clear that poverty has entered the middle class that now sees itself knocking at the door of social services departments. The dead ends of mainstream social work are now more than apparent. People have no money to pay the bills, their rent and so on, and casework (or 'social work with individuals', as it is often called in Greece) has no significant effect on people's lives. It can be used as a relief and/or as the 'breakwater' of people's anger against the system.[5]

However, social work can choose another way. In my opinion, social work needs to get out of the office (both in academia and in social service departments) and get involved in the community. There is a crucial need for more creative and effective interventions by social work. There is a crucial need for social work to take action in these forms of resistance that have been developed by and with the people who suffer and resist.

While this response was being written there were daily attacks by fascists on immigrants in Greece. The rise of fascism in Greece, as well as in other European countries, is another indicator that social work needs to raise its voice. In this advocacy of human rights, social work is not alone. There are many activists, anti-racists and political organisations, initiatives of citizens, academics and so on. It's an opportunity, as Jones and Novak mention, for social work to 'be part of the solution and not part of the problem.

Notes

[1] For example, during the first three months of 2010 unemployment rose significantly compared with the corresponding period in 2009. Specifically, from January to March 2009, the official percentage was reported as 9.3% while for the same period in 2010 it was 11.7% (National Statistical Services, 2010, p 2). According to the National Statistical Services in December 2011 unemployment affected 21.0% of the working-age population, while the GSEE (Greek General Confederation of Labour) calculates the real unemployment rate to be 25.0% of the population (www.gsee.gr/news/news_view.php?id=1770).

[2] The anti-immigration policy of the EU and Greek state has led to migrants being blamed for unemployment, crime and cuts. Thus has increased anti-immigrant sentiments amongst some in Greek society and created a space for fascist organisations such as Golden Dawn to exploit. It comes as no surprise that in Greek elections of 6 May

2013 the fascists raised their percentage of the vote and entered the Greek parliament.

[3] The recent publication of photos of prostitutes with HIV by state services in Greece caused reactions from a number of Greek organisations (feminists, activists, health professionals; see http:// positivevoicegr.blogspot.com/2012/04/blog-post_30.html) as well as the Greek Union for Human Rights (www.hlhr.gr/details. php?id=670) and Greek Social Work Action Network (http:// socialworkaction.wordpress.com/2012/05/18/%CE%BA%CF%81% CE%B1%CF%84%CE%B9%CE%BA%CF%8C%CF%82-%CF%81 %CE%B1%CF%84%CF%83%CE%B9%CF%83%CE%BC%CF%8C %CF%82-%CE%BA%CE%B1%CE%B9-%CF%86%CF%84%CF%8 E%CF%87%CE%B5%CE%B9%CE%B1-e%CF%80%CE%B9%CE %BA%CE%AF%CE%BD/).

[4] See the Greek network's site at http://socialworkaction.wordpress. com/

[5] See the video concerning social work and austerity in Greece (in English) on SWAN's site: www.socialworkfuture.org/articles-and-analysis/international-articles/235-greece-2012-social-work-in-austerity and at https://vimeo.com/39398286

Now time for neoliberalism: resisting Plan B from below

Sanford F. Schram

The time is now for mass mobilisation. We see it everywhere across the globe, as Chris Jones and Tony Novak point out. And it is about time. The fact of the matter is that most people would rather not be political, not risk losing what they already have, and not take their chances engaging in direct action. So when they do, we know something has happened to change the normal course of affairs. Once people come to see that there is less to lose by acting, they are ready to be mobilised. And that is a good thing since, as Frances Fox Piven and Richard Cloward once famously said: 'A placid poor get nothing, but a turbulent poor sometimes get something' (1971, p 38). Their point is that the historical record is clear that the only proven way to get real change is at those times when the people on the bottom rise up and say they are mad as hell and are not going to take it any more. The global economic meltdown since the onset of the Great Recession in 2008 has created the crucible in which the new uprising has mushroomed. From the Occupy Wall Street movement to mass demonstrations in cities across the globe in reaction to inequitable economic policies, those marginalised and left by the wayside by the resultant global economic restructuring are finally fighting back.

And it is not just the poor. As Guy Standing (2011) has noted, there is a new precariat. Actually several. In addition to the poor, whose precarity is persistent, now we see those marginalised by the hollowing-out of the middle class joining forces with those already deemed as disposable populations to rage against the system. This has been a long time in coming. Economic restructuring has not happened overnight. Instead, it has come incrementally with economic

—

downturns successively presenting opportunities to offload workers, outsource jobs and restructure firms so that they can more efficiently and profitably, if also more heartlessly, participate in the global economy. For instance, for four of the five US recessions since the recession of 1970, each time the economy recovered it came back with fewer jobs than before, a result most likely due to major corporations seizing the opportunity to not bring back laid-off workers so as to allow for a restructured firm in each case to move further into the global economy where first-world workers are an uncompetitive burden (Cauchon, 2011). This would not necessarily be fatal for sustaining an occupational structure that could enable most workers to earn a decent living for themselves and their families. Yet, that would require systematic planning to move laid-off workers into new jobs that paid decent wages. Instead, in the US most especially, but increasingly now elsewhere, the state's role in responding to restructuring is insufficient to keep pace. One looming sign of this crisis situation is that wages have been stagnant for most classes of workers for over 30 years now, with manual skilled workers seeing major diminutions in the real value of their pay (Mishel, 2012). Precarity is pervasive for all except the uppermost in the class system.

The battle playing out in the political realm in advanced capitalist societies is whether the state any longer has an obligation towards the mass of working people who are being systematically marginalised by the intensification of restructuring that is occurring in the current post-Great Recession period. In the US, there is the distinct possibility of moving to a tiered society. At the top, there is a limited stratum of upper- and upper-middle-class people, ensconced in positions of corporate oversight and needed professional occupations. At the bottom is everyone else, who are increasingly deemed as not deserving of the state's attention, in part because they failed to position themselves as successful participants for the globalising economy and are, as a result, seen as a burden that a globally competitive corporate sector cannot and will not carry. At the extreme, those in poverty are cast aside as disposable populations of one or another sort who are to be monitored, surveilled, disciplined and punished more than they are to be helped.

—

Jodi Dean captures this dynamic as expressed in 2012 presidential campaign rhetoric:

> What will we see in 20 years (or earlier)? The amplification of the worst trends already present in our society: the super-rich sheltered in their gated communities and high-rises, defended by the military (inclusive of a militarized police) and their own private security forces. Private education would continue to educate their children. Private health care would ensure their health and longevity.
>
> What about the rest of us? We will be free. Free to fight among ourselves – completely armed – for the scraps that remain. We will compete for scholarships – ostensibly proving the continuation of merit and opportunity. We will compete for grants for art, design, and various other sorts of contracts. We will work ever harder for ever less as public schools, roads, hospitals, and infrastructure decline. And when we resist, when we organize – the defense budget Ryan has secured will fund the drone warfare and surveillance used against us. Private prisons will provide housing. (Dean, 2012)

Dean is onto something that has implications for the helping professions as well as everyone else. It is here at this neoliberal terminus we find a transformed social work, depoliticised and refocused on managing disposable populations. Social work no longer stands outside power but now is more than ever thoroughly assimilated to it. Across a wide variety of populations in need of various forms of assistance and treatment, social work shifts to technologies of the state, forms of governmentality, practices associated with getting served populations to internalise an ethic of self-discipline and personal responsibility so that they will handle their own problems as best they can on their own, become less of burden for the constrained state and more willing to take up whatever limited positions in the globalising economy that they are afforded. Social work increasingly is comprised of forms of 'psy' services focused on helping to realise the disciplinary demands of the neoliberalising state, which is now ever more dedicated to managing rather than serving disposable populations. When examining changes across a number of different areas of human service provision today, most striking are the parallel shifts in treatment towards a more disciplinary approach to managing service populations (Schram and Silverman, 2012). It is the end of social work as we knew it.

This disciplinary regime is part and parcel of what is being called neoliberalism. Yet, neoliberalism is actually the corporate Plan B for the state. Neoliberalism is, for me and my collaborators, not simply an ideology that prizes market fundamentalism and seeks a return to laissez-faire economics (Soss et al, 2011). That would be Plan A. Yet, Plan A has run afoul of Keynesian economics and its insistence that only the state is big enough to counteract market failure. Though often repudiated by the Right, Keynesianism has remained a point of contention since the Great Depression of the 1930s until now in the time of the Great Recession. As result, there remains a belief in the welfare state to counter the capriciousness of the market and the adversity it creates for those who get marginalised. As a result, the proponents of neoliberalism cannot just sweep the welfare state away and return to a system of laissez-faire economics such as that which reigned in the 19th century and the age of the robber barons. Instead, the right must resort to Plan B: if you cannot eradicate the welfare state, the next best thing is to marketise it. Plan B involves remaking welfare state programmes to operate consonant with market principles in the service of more efficiently buttressing the market itself. From education vouchers to medical insurance vouchers to private investments accounts in lieu of social security, from welfare-to-work programmes grounded in incentivising taking up low-wage work to the penalties and rewards in drug treatment programmes, the programmes of the welfare state are increasingly run structured according to strict market logic only to get clients to be more market-compliant actors themselves. The state increasingly contracts with for-profit providers who are incentivised to discipline their clients so that those clients themselves become more disciplined and docile, internalising market logic so they will more willing accept the verdict of the globalising market and take any low-wage jobs, if available, as their main source of economic salvation.[1]

Social workers are increasingly involved in neoliberalised service provision that features this sort of disciplinary work imposed on themselves that they then must in turn impose on their clients. Yet, all is not lost. Neoliberalisation is a failed project, where vouchers do not cover the cost of market participation for schools or health care, where incentives for work still lead to poverty-inuring low-wage and insecure employment, where addicts are incentivised but still also very often remain poor, without work and often homeless. Re-entry programs for ex-felons go the same way. Private accounts for social security retirement investments are likely to come up short as well. As more and more people become marginalised, as the lower tier grows, as people see they are left on the outside holding an empty bag, the willingness to go political, to take direct action, to rise from below will increase. Neoliberalisation of the welfare state will not stand. Change will come, from below; and we will be better for it. Globalisation be damned.

Note

[1] Now even Wall Street is encouraged to invest in 'social impact bonds' that promise capital gains if programmes funded achieve performance goals. See Chen (2012).

What are you going to do about it?

Chris Jones and Tony Novak

It is gratifying to see that all the respondents broadly endorsed our principal arguments and demands. All of them, from their varying societies and countries, describe the terror and damage of unbridled neoliberalism and its devastation of lives and well-being, especially among the most downtrodden and vulnerable. They all note similar patterns and social and economic trends, as what Schram rightly calls disposable populations grow in size, inequalities between the wealthiest and the rest widen and deepen, and as the state responses to welfare, crime and protest become ever more authoritarian and disciplinary. In general terms, in many of the core capitalist societies, such as the US, the UK and Canada, the overall trajectory of the state today is more concerned with minimising costs, social control, management and discipline, rather than seeking to ameliorate the problems of poverty and unemployment. The extraordinary increases in incarceration and surveillance of the population provide stark examples both of the contemporary neoliberal state's orientation to its own people and the mining of corporate profits on the backs of the most disadvantaged. For the poorest, the agents of social control and the gatekeepers of declining resources are now as likely to wear the outfits of a private corporation as they are the uniforms of the police or the prison service.

The concept of *contradiction* has been a long-held tenet of critical welfare state analysis, and in this book Abramowitz classically sets out the manner in which the state's welfare measures are simultaneously good and bad for people. As social workers know well, service usersoften appreciate and need state services yet despise the manner in which they are allocated (such as humiliating and stigmatising assessment processes) and the inadequacy of the resources available. For many progressive workers in state welfare an implicit daily aspect of their work has involved and does involve exploring the spaces and opportunities the contradictions of state welfare open up for humane practice. A UK publication from the 1970s entitled *In and against the state* (London Edinburgh Weekend Return Group, 1980[1]), which was the product of the work of a range of engaged state welfare professionals from social workers to housing officers and academics, offers an outstanding example of this kind of activity. This publication reflected the perspectives of many British radicals in arguing that the emergence of a post-war social democratic consensus, especially in Europe and Canada and to a lesser degree in the US, offered countless spaces *within* the state for meaningful progressive work with clients and service users. *In and against the state* became for many of our generation a kind of handbook which both confirmed our feelings that we could do something valuable even when working for the enemy and that the structures and process of state welfare could be manipulated for working-class gain.

But as we have seen throughout all the contributions, although the concept of contradiction is still meaningful it has not remained unchanged. Neoliberalism in sweeping away social democratic welfare forms has transformed the nature of contradiction in this area. To put it bluntly, welfare state workers and professions of all sorts have experienced at least three decades of declining space in which to operate humanely and progressively. From Greece to Canada, with variation in intensity, the same processes have been unfolding whereby state workers and their user constituencies have been subject to almost perpetual interference and restraint. The result is that in many societies their welfare systems are far less contradictory, offer far fewer opportunities for progressive practice and are simply more punitive and restrictive. It has been and remains a process which has not just been about reducing the amount of welfare provided to the people but has also involved transforming the 'ways of welfare'.

—

As a consequence, welfare state agencies have been subject to unparalleled reform and change over the past three decades. There has been a veritable cascade of legislation that has subjected all major areas of provision from education, health and social care to prisons to processes of continual change. It has been a process which has washed tsunami-like over all the major state-sponsored professions from teachers to social workers. With respect to the social professions the neoliberal mantra of them having too much autonomy and too little oversight has been one of the drumbeats of recent history. Professional self-regulation has been replaced by new configurations that have elevated the manager over the profession and ushered in a deluge of forms, permissions and procedures that now shape and determine state interventions. Professional autonomy and judgement have been ridiculed as the preserve of the self-interested. The message has been insistent and consistent; welfare professionals are not to be trusted. They are self-serving and off (the neoliberal) message.

But while we should worry over these developments we should not mourn the decline of social democratic welfare. It was never enough in either quality or quantity, and in any event the privileging of professionals over service users and clients was and remains profoundly undemocratic. The old dominant forms offer us little and there is little to be gained from seeking to return (even if we could) to that place. Equally, however, we need to shift our thinking and it is simply no longer viable to think of state welfare in the ways we did at the time of *In and against the state*. In particular, we need to recognise that the contradictory spaces offered by social democratic welfare just don't exist or have been severely curtailed in the neoliberal state.

In different ways these shifts are illustrated in the responses to our opening essay. All of the respondents point to the ways in which official social work in their countries has changed for the worse. They talk of an official social work that has been routinised and bureaucratised and subject to extensive managerial controls. They speak of an official social work that is traumatised and silenced. They allude to a social work where, as in the case of Greece in the midst of the most brutal

—

55

humanitarian crisis, it has no takers because everyone knows that state social workers have nothing to offer and it may even place them at risk.

While Greece may represent an extreme case it is evident that official social work in this neoliberal world is in a mess; it has little to offer its service users and clients; it is a miserable place to be a worker and it has a history of capitulation to the state. Never the strongest and most respected of state-sponsored professions, official social work despite this fundamental weakness has been exceptionally pathetic in its resistance to these developments. Dudziak and Teloni are both right to draw attention to the utter feebleness of official social work to make any significant stand to fight or resist the neoliberal onslaught. In its mainstream professional organisations as well as in the universities and social work agencies we are faced with capitulation after capitulation. As Dudziak observed, it seemed that any criticism of these damaging developments was considered internally as constituting unprofessional conduct and disloyalty. This is not just true for Canada. There is a story still waiting to be written of the collusion of the leaders of official social work with neoliberalism, which is a story not only of cowardice and lack of political judgement but more fundamentally a shameful story of official social work's abandonment of its service users and clients.

State social work has for too long claimed to be the sole guardian of and domain for social work. Its tutelage has seen the activity gutted and transformed with little left that even the most die-hard casework traditionalists would distinguish as social work. The time has surely come for us to at least choose the right words to describe what passes as official social work as in fact 'community surveillance and rationing'. This work may pay the rent but the real challenge now is to break the mindset that says that the only place to do social work is in the state and to destroy the illusion that there is sufficient space to work as a progressive in today's official social work. This is only true for a tiny minority and largely due to local reasons. The neoliberal state offers increasingly little space for manoeuvre.

Given this context and the neoliberalisation of official social work in many key societies we believe that we should seriously consider Teloni's call for social work academics and front-line practitioners to leave their offices and their desks to spend more time with and alongside the emerging social movements of the poor. Teloni and other similar social work activists, especially evident in the growing Social Work Action Network, are making this call in part because they believe that social workers can make a positive contribution to the struggles for justice and humanity. Here we are not talking of the ersatz social work of the state, but a social work with a much longer pedigree rooted in solidarity, compassion and understanding. It is the kind of social work that Michael Lavalette and Chris Jones witnessed in the Palestinian refugee camps in the West Bank, where young people were enthusiastically undertaking new social work courses at their universities because they saw in their values and methods ways of making a difference (Jones and Lavalette, 2011). Popular social work such as we saw in the West Bank, which was helping children and their friends and families overcome traumas such as nightmares, bed-wetting and mutism caused directly by the Israeli occupation, made a difference. First and foremost, it helped the direct casualties rebuild their confidence and deal with the trauma. Secondly, it opened up the issue of childhood trauma being a consequence of occupation and not a private matter to be dealt with (or not) in the family. Over the course of our visits, interest and initiatives to deal with the psychosocial impact of the occupation on young people were growing, especially with respect to the children who had been arrested, interrogated, tortured and imprisoned. Social work is now being developed and added to the tools of resistance.

But social work will never become a force of progressive change or resistance if it remains wedded to the state. Of that we can be certain. Only in the hands of the people can social work ever be true to its ideals and values. So it is time for new strong words and new strong actions. Too many state social workers seem defeated and dismayed by their experiences. In no small measure this is the fault of social work education, which fails again and again to provide students with a social and political perspective that can begin to make sense of the world they confront and experience. Their courses invariably lead them to hopelessness and helplessness, which is hardly surprising given the lack of intellectual rigour. What else can one expect from a social work academy that has prostituted itself to the demands of state employers? Be that as it may, social and economic conditions are now so extreme that we have every right to demand more, much more, of social workers, their profession and their agencies and ask new questions not only including 'whose side are you on?', but also 'what are you going to do about it?'.

Note

[1] The original A4 book was published in 1978 and republished with minor changes by Pluto in 1980.

References

Abramovitz, M. (2004) 'Saving capitalism from itself: whither the welfare state?', *New England Journal of Public Policy*, vol 20, no 1, pp 21–32.

Ali, M. (2011) *State of the dream 2011:. Austerity for whom?*, United for a Fair Economy, 14 January, 14, available at www.faireconomy.org/files/State_of_the_Dream_2011.pdf

Anderson, P. (2011) 'Lula's Brazil', *London Review of Books*, vol 33, no 7, 31 March, pp 3–12.

Aronowitz, S. (2011) 'One, two, many Madisons: the war on public sector workers', *New Labor Forum* vol 20, no 2 (Spring), pp 15–21.

Bageant, J. (2008) *Deer hunting with Jesus*, London: Portobello Books.

Bamfield, L. (2005) ' Making the public case for tackling poverty and inequality', *Poverty* no 121, Summer, www.cpag.org.uk/info/Povertyarticles/Poverty121/making.htm#note3 (accessed 3 January 2012).

Campbell, B. (2012) 'Canada's Dutch disease', Editorial, *CCPA Monitor*, July/August, p 2.

Campbell, N.D. (2011) House GOP Spending Cuts Will Devastate Women, Families, and Economy," *The Hill*, 16 February, http://thehill.com/blogs/congress-blog/economy-a-budget/144585-house-gop-spending-cuts-will-devastate-women-families-and-economy.

Cauchon, D. (2011) 'Job creation limps along after recession', *USA Today*, 20 May.

CCPA (Canadian Centre for Policy Alternatives) (2012) 'Hunger in Canada', *CCPA Monitor*, July/August, p 2.

Center on Budget and Policy Priorities (nd) 'What is driving the large projected deficits?', www.cbpp.org/research/index.cfm?fa=topic&id=121

Chen, D. (2012) 'Goldman to invest in city jail program, profiting if recidivism falls sharply', *New York Times*, 2 August.

Davis, M. (2007) *Evil paradises: Dreamworlds of neoliberalism*, The New Press, New York.

Dean, J. (2012) 'Paul Ryan has a 20 year plan to destroy the government. Where's ours?', I cite website, available at: http://jdeanicite.typepad.com/i_cite/2012/08/paul-ryan-has-a-20-year-plan-to-destroy-the-government-wheres-ours.html.

Engels, F (1845/2009) *The conditions of the English working class* (reissued edition), Oxford World Classics, Oxford: OUP.

Feiner, S. (2011) 'Scott Walker Undoes Decades of Women's History', 29 March, available at www.womensenews.org/story/commentary/110328/scott-walker-undoes-decades-womens-history.

Fox Piven, F. and Cloward, R.A. (1971) *Regulating the poor: The functions of public welfare*, New York: Vintage Books.

Fox Piven, F. and Cloward, R. (1972) *Regulating the poor*, London: Tavistock Publications.

Georgetti, K. (2012) 'Ottawa bullying unemployed workers in Atlantic Canada', Opinion editorial, *Halifax Chronicle Herald*, 24 May.

Greenstein, R. (2012) 'CBO shows Ryan budget would set nation on path to end most of government other than social security, health care, and defense by 2050', Center on Budget and Policy Priorities, March, www.cbpp.org/cms/index.cfm?fa=view&id=3708

Greenstein, R. and Kogan, R. (2012) 'Are low-income programs enlarging the nation's long-term fiscal problem?', Center on Budget and Policy Priorities, May, www.cbpp.org/cms/index.cfm?fa=view&id=3772

Guttmacher Institute (2012) 'State policy trends: abortion and contraception in the crosshairs', 13 April, www.guttmacher.org/media/inthenews/2012/04/13/index.html

Hallsworth, S. and Brotherton, D. (2011) *Urban disorder and gangs: A critique and a warning*, London: Runnymede Trust.

Jones, C. (1983) *State social work and the working class*, Basingstoke: Macmillan.

Jones, C. (2001) 'Voices from the front line: state social workers and New Labour', *British Journal of Social Work*, vol 31, no 4, pp 547–62.

—

Jones, C. and Lavalette, M. (2011) 'Popular social work in the Palestinian West Bank: dispatches from the front line', in M. Lavalette and V. Ioakimidis (eds) *Social work in extremis: Lessons for social work internationally*, Bristol: Policy Press.

Jones, C. and Novak, T. (1999) *Poverty, welfare and disciplinary state*, London: Routledge.

Jones, O. (2011) *Chavs: The demonization of the working class*, London: Verso.

Klein, N. (2007) *The shock doctrine: The rise of disaster capitalism*, New York: Metropolitan Books.

Laborers' International Union of North America (2011) 'Women hit hardest by attacks on public sector unions', 5 February, available at www.liunawomen.org/women-hit-hardest-by-attacks-on-publicsector.

Langille, D. (2010) 'Facts about the working poor in Canada', 11 January, available at: http://poornomore.ca blog.

London Edinburgh Weekend Return Group (1980) *In and against the state*, London: Pluto Press.

Macdonald, D. (2012) 'Canada's banks lavished with $114 billion in government aid', *CCPA Monitor*, May, p 1.

Merrick, K. and Horney, J. (2012) 'Chairman Ryan gets 62 percent of his huge budget cuts from programs for lower-income Americans', Center on Budget and Policy Priorities, March, www.cbpp.org/cms/index.cfm?fa=view&id=3723.

Minton, A. (2009) *Ground control*, London: Penguin Books.

Mishel, L. (2012) 'The wedges between productivity and median compensation growth', Issue Brief # 330, 26 April, Washington, DC: Economic Policy Institute.

Mooney, G. and Lavalette, M. (eds) (2000) *Class struggle and social welfare*, London: Taylor and Francis.

National Women's Law Center (2011a) 'House Republican spending cuts in HR1 devastating to women, families, and the economy', Washington, DC: National Women's Law Center, 30 March, available at: www.nwlc.org/resource/house-republican-spending-cuts-hr-1-devastating-women-families-and-economy.

National Women's Law Center (2011b) 'Women's stake in the battle over public employees' collective bargaining rights', Washington, DC: National Women's Law Center, available at: www.nwlc.org/resource/womens-stake-battle-over-public-employees-collective-bargaining-rights.

National Women's Law Center (2012) 'Modest recovery beginning for women', April, Washington, DC: National Women's Law Center, available at: http://www.nwlc.org/resource/modest-recovery-beginning-women.

Novak, T. (1988) *Poverty and the state*, Milton Keynes; Open University Press.

O'Reilly, A.M. and Clark, W. (2011) 'All work and no pay: the rise of Workfare', *Red Pepper Blog*, November, www.redpepper.org.uk/all-work-and-no-pay/ (accessed 26 November 2011).

Pitts, S. (2011) *Black workers and the public sector,* Berkeley, CA: Center for Labor Research and Education, University of California, 4 April, available at: http://laborcenter.berkeley.edu/blackworkers/blacks_public_sector11.pdf.

Pollack, E. (2012) 'Ryan budget cuts would cost jobs', 21 March, available at: www.epi.org/blog/paul-ryan-budget-discretionary-cuts-cost-jobs/.

Rebick, J. (2005) *Ten thousand roses: The making of a feminist revolution*, Toronto: Penguin Canada.

Schram, S.F. and Silverman, B. (2012) 'The end of social work: neoliberalizing social policy implementation', *Critical Policy Studies*, vol 6, no 2, pp 128–45, available at: http://dx.doi.org/10.1080/19460171.2012.689734.

Soss, J., Fording, R.C. and Schram, S.F. (2011) *Disciplining the poor: neoliberal paternalism and the persistent power of race* (Chicago: University of Chicago Press.

Standing, G. (2011) *The precariat: The new dangerous class*, New York: Bloomsbury USA.

Stanford, J. (1998) 'The rise and fall of deficit-mania', in W. Antony and L. Samuelson (eds) *Power and resistance: Critical thinking about social issues*, 2nd edn, Halifax: Fernwood Publishing.

—

Stedman Jones, G. (1971) *Outcast London*, Oxford: Clarendon Press.

Swanson, J. (2001) *Poor-bashing: The politics of exclusion*, Toronto: Between the Lines.

Teeple, G. and McBride, S. (eds) (2011) *Relations of global power: Neoliberal order and disorder*, Toronto: University of Toronto Press Inc.

Toronto Star (2012) 'Broadbent poll uncovers public desire to close inequality gap', Opinion editorial, 9 April.

Turner, J. (2011) 'As many pairs of shoes as she likes', *London Review of Books,* 15 December, pp 11–15.

US Department of Labor, Bureau of Labor Statistics (2011) 'Union members – 2010', available at: http://www.bls.gov/news.release/pdf/union2.pdf

US Department of Agriculture, Food and Nutrition Service (2011) Special Supplemental Nutrition Program for Women, Infants and Children (WIC)', 31 October, www.fns.usda.gov/pd/37WIC_Monthly.htm

Vygotsky, L. (1934/1986) *Thought and language*, newly revised edn, ed A. Kozulin, Cambridge, MA: MIT Press.

Wilkinson, R. (2005) *The impact of inequalities: How to make sick societies healthier*, London: Routledge.

Wilkinson, R. and Pickett, K. (2010) *The spirit level: Why equality is better for everyone*, London: Penguin.